DUNDEE REFLECTIONS

Photography by David Springford

Published by More Than Image

Design & Production by David Springford
ISBN 978-0-9566573-1-2

Printed and bound in Musselburgh
by Ivanhoe Printing Company Ltd.

PHOTOGRAPHER DAVID SPRINGFORD

David's interest in photography began with his first SLR camera, a reconditioned Pentax ME Super. His passion and talent for it further developed while working as a graphic designer in a variety of media, including print, web and screen.

His eclectic collection of limited edition prints of Dundee features angles and reflections, towers and turrets, clouds and curves.

Although born and bred in Edinburgh, David lived for several years in Dundee whilst studying at Duncan of Jordanstone College of Art and Design. David portrays a more oblique view of familiar tourist attractions and captures the less-well-known in close-up. What is important is the part each plays in the composition to see Dundee in a new light.

Limited edition fine art prints of the images in this book, as well as others, including his Edinburgh Reflections Collection, are available online at David's website www.infinityphotos.co.uk

DUNDEE REFLECTIONS

David photographed his entire Dundee collection using only a Leica M8.2 Rangefinder camera with 50mm (Summicron-M 1:2/50) lens.

This added to the challenge to capture and compose each subject, taking into account most would be cropped to 1x1 ratio.

DUNDEE

Dundee tightly hugs one side of the open Firth of Tay. The city links hands with the Kingdom of Fife via road and rail bridges across the estuary's silvery waters.

Dundee has emerged strongly from its maritime and industrial heritage as a city at the forefront of 21st century cultural, artistic and scientific life. Quays and docks, once centres for whaling and shipbuilding, are now home to chic hotels and penthouse apartments.

From firm foundations built on jute, jam and journalism, Dundee presently leads the way in biomedical advances and digital entertainment. This is a city moving purposely forward, both proud and mindful of its past.

Firth of Tay from Dundee Law

VICTORIA DOCK/CITY QUAY

Victoria Dock was in its day one of Scotland's largest enclosed docks. Now used as a marina, it forms part of Dundee's City Quay regeneration development. Both HMS Frigate Unicorn, the oldest British-built ship afloat anywhere in the world, and the former North Carr lightship are permanently anchored in the dock.

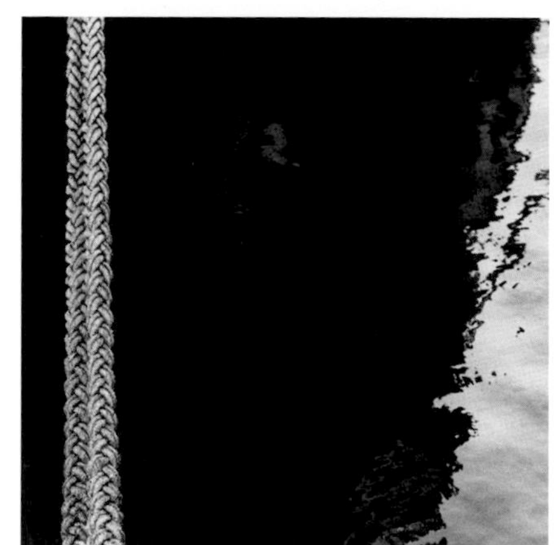

1½ TONS

BAXTER PARK

Baxter Park takes its name from Victorian jute baron, David Baxter. He and his sisters commissioned Sir Joseph Paxton, the leading designer of the day, and gifted the park to the people of Dundee in 1863. The park was recently restored to its original Victorian design and remains Scotland's only complete Paxton park.

DUNDEE LAW

This mound of volcanic rock is probably Dundee's most prominent landmark. Its lofty position has served as Pictish hill fort and Roman lookout post. Today it's the ideal vantage point for views across the city, countryside and coast to Fife, Perthshire and beyond.

Tay Rail Bridge from Dundee Law

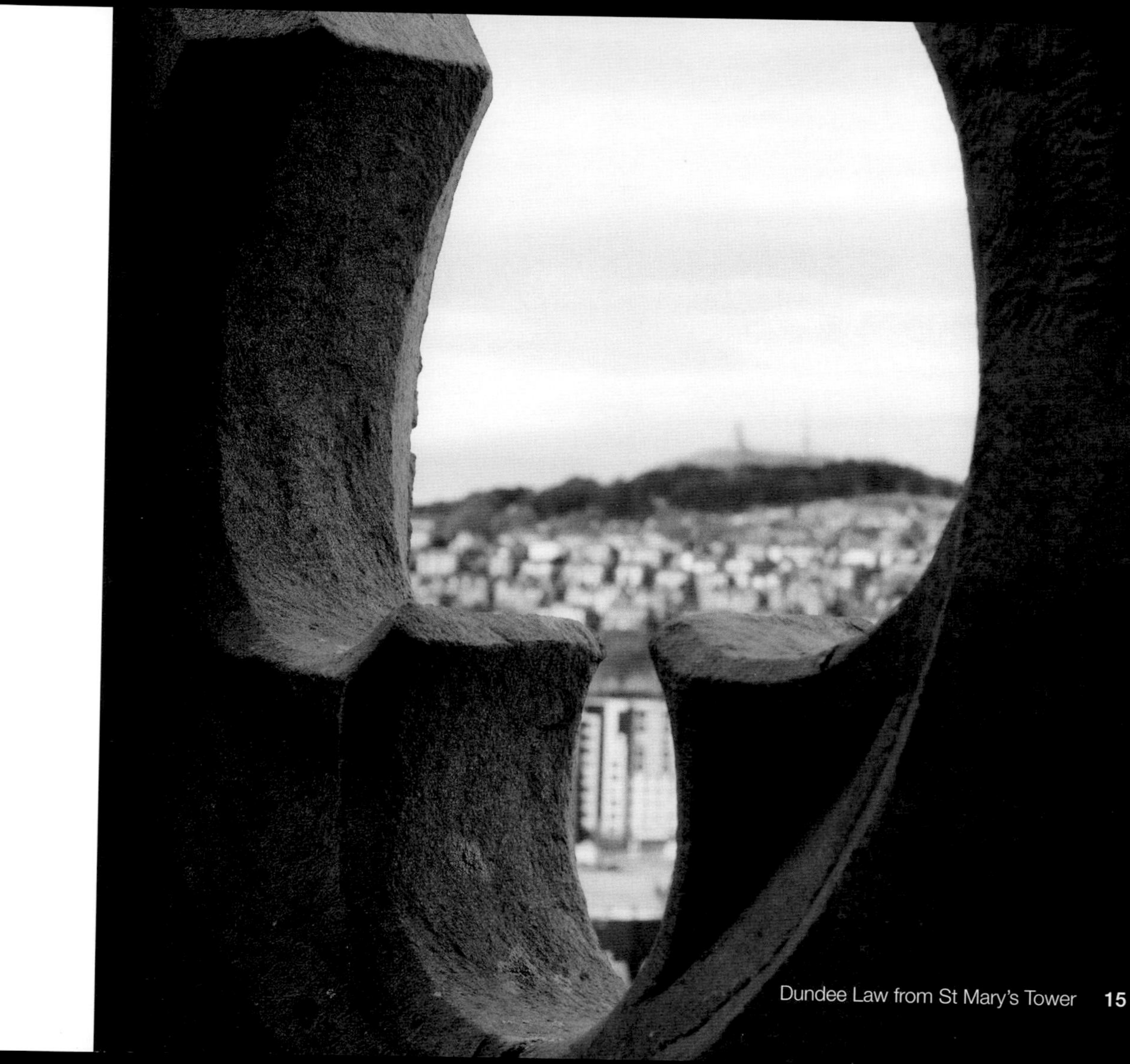

Dundee Law from St Mary's Tower

BALGAY PARK

Balgay Park was initially created to help improve the health of Victorian mill workers. The open public space proved a welcome and necessary respite from the workers' poor living and working conditions.

Feel the benefit yourself along the park's mature woodland paths with views across the River Tay.

Cox's Stack from Balgay Park

MILLS OBSERVATORY

Britain's only full-time public observatory sits within Balgay Park. It was gifted to the people of Dundee in 1935, thanks to a bequest from John Mills, a local manufacturer and keen amateur scientist.

Mills Observatory upholds its original aim to this day: to encourage the public understanding of science.

Mills Observatory

Lochee Park

Tay Rail Bridge from Mills Observatory

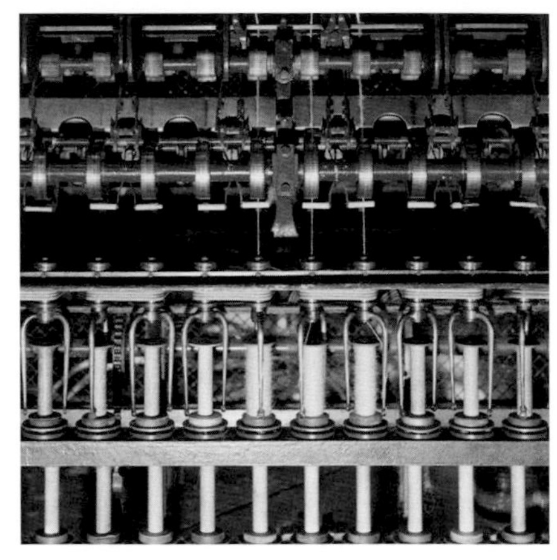

 Verdant Works machinery

VERDANT WORKS

More than a century ago, Dundee became the world's leading centre for the production of jute and flax.

This finely-woven tale of international success and working hardships is cleverly and evocatively retold through restored machinery and modern multimedia.

CAMPERDOWN PARK

Dundee's largest public park owes its name to a naval victory off the Dutch coast in 1797 at the Battle of Camperdown. The neo-classical house in the grounds was the rather grand home of the triumphant Admiral Adam Duncan.

Camperdown now embraces a wooded haven for wildlife, a reservoir, wildlife centre, fun fair, playground and golf courses.

Cox's Stack from Camperdown Park

COX'S STACK. CAMPERDOWN WORKS

Dundee may no longer produce jute but the structures of the industry's heyday remain. Cox's Stack is named after the three brothers who owned what was at the time the world's largest jute mill.

Its unusual form of an Italian bell tower or campanile captures the essence of the Victorian industrial age. To this day it is the tallest chimney in Scotland at 282 feet.

MAGGIE'S CENTRE

Maggie's Dundee occupies a peaceful spot within the grounds of Ninewells, Dundee's teaching hospital. This was the UK's third such centre dedicated to helping people cope with cancer.

It was the first new-build Maggie's Centre as well as the first building in the UK by renowned architect, Frank Gehry, a close friend of Maggie. Artist Antony Gormley donated his sculpture Another Time X to stand in the grounds.

Antony Gormley sculpture

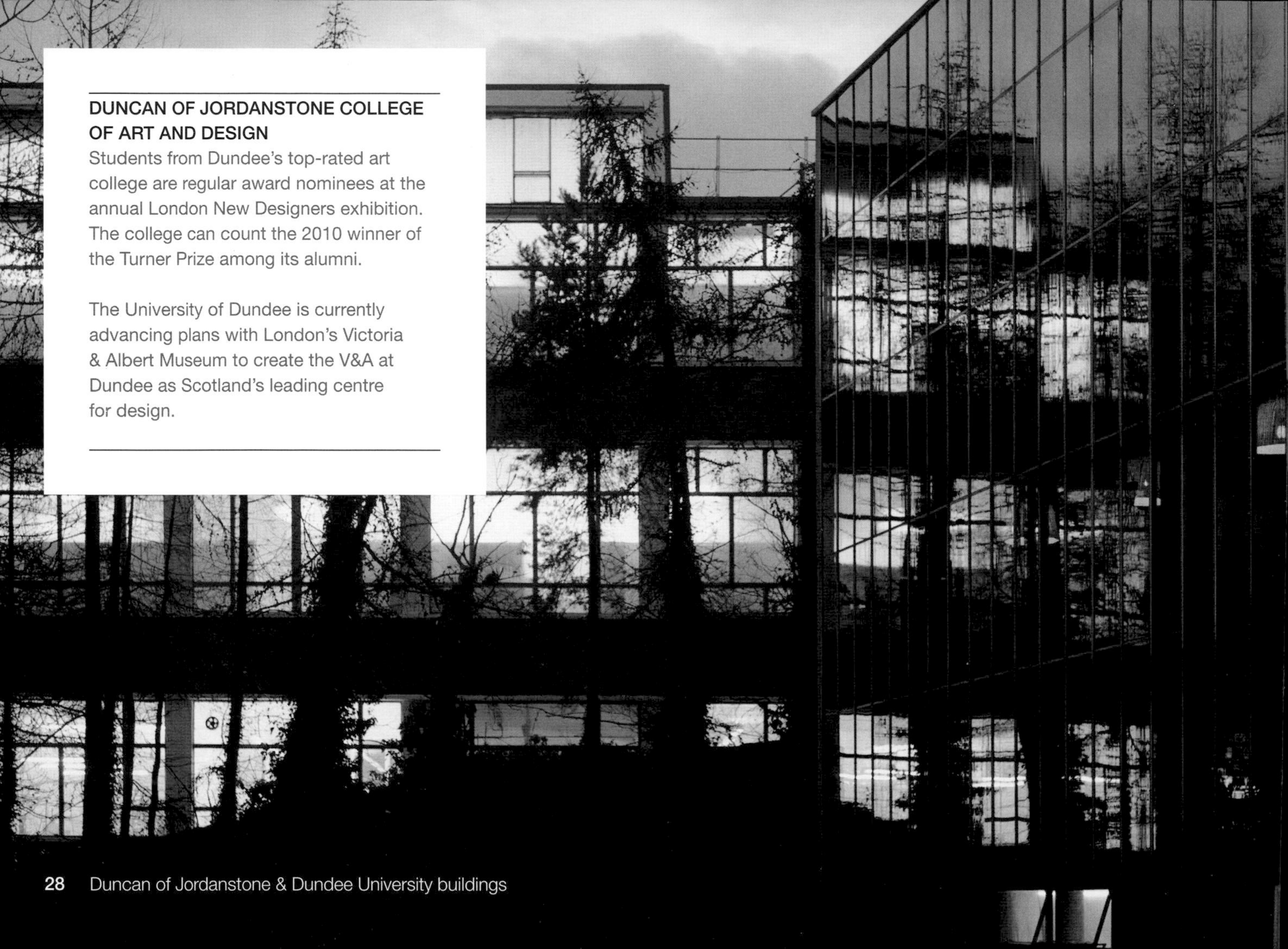

DUNCAN OF JORDANSTONE COLLEGE OF ART AND DESIGN

Students from Dundee's top-rated art college are regular award nominees at the annual London New Designers exhibition. The college can count the 2010 winner of the Turner Prize among its alumni.

The University of Dundee is currently advancing plans with London's Victoria & Albert Museum to create the V&A at Dundee as Scotland's leading centre for design.

THE HOWFF

Howff is an old Scots word for 'meeting place'. It seems a rather strange name for a graveyard. However the site was previously where the Nine Trades of Dundee would meet in the sixteenth century.

It's Dundee's oldest surviving cemetery, the final resting place of many of the city's prominent sons and daughters right up to the mid 19th century. Among them is James Chalmers, inventor of the adhesive postage stamp.

MAGDALEN GREEN PARK

The city's oldest park has been enjoyed by Dundonians for more than 400 years. The park's Victorian bandstand quickly became a Dundee landmark. A recent spruce-up has ensured the bandstand's continued appeal for summer concerts on Sunday afternoons.

Bandstand

View of Firth of Tay from Dundee Airport

DUNDEE AIRPORT

Dundee Airport took off in the Sixties at the same time as the construction of the Tay Road Bridge.

Scheduled flights from London, Birmingham and Belfast bring golfers tantalisingly close to St Andrews and other championship courses. As well as a local flying school, scenic helicopter tours from the airport make the most of the Scottish scenery.

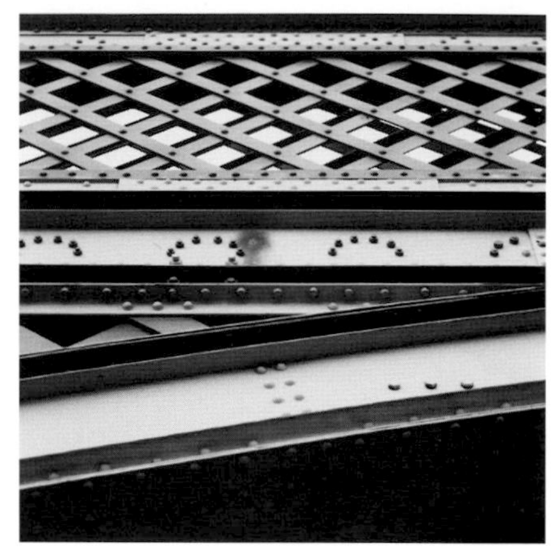

TAY RAIL BRIDGE

When it opened in 1878, it was the longest bridge in the world. People from around the globe flocked to see this feat of engineering.

A year later the bridge failed one stormy night as a train was crossing with the loss of 75 lives. You can still see the original masonry piers standing in the river in the shadow of the robust replacement bridge built in 1887.

TAY ROAD BRIDGE

Car ferries made way for road bridges in the 1960s as Fife connected with Dundee and Edinburgh across the Tay and Forth estuaries. Originally a toll bridge, traffic now flows unhindered in and out of Dundee's city centre.

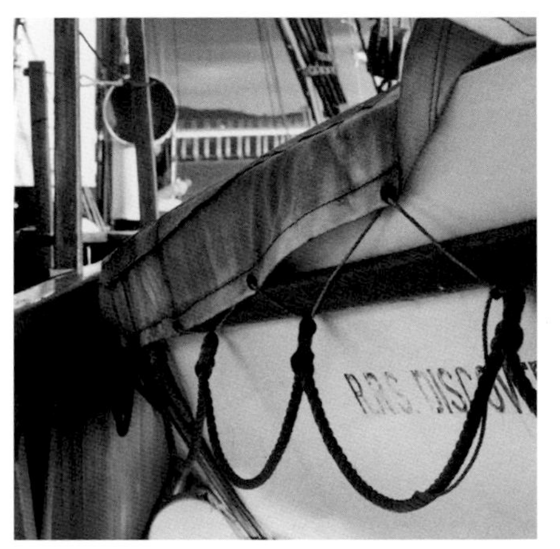

Tay Road Bridge from RSS Discovery and St Mary's Tower

RRS DISCOVERY

The ship that famously took Captain Scott to the Antarctic was built in Dundee's shipyards. RRS Discovery was the first vessel constructed specifically to undertake scientific research. Dundee's expertise in building whaling ships ensured Discovery was up to the tortuous trip.

Now berthed permanently in Dundee, the ship bears witness to the courage of Scott and his crew.

Tay Rail Bridge from RSS Discovery

ST MARY'S TOWER

This 15th century tower, known locally as The Old Steeple, is Dundee's oldest surviving building. Over the centuries it's been used as a prison, a clock-tower, a belfry and a watch-tower. It's an energetic 232 steps to the top.

The Old Steeple

Tay Rail Bridge from The Old Steeple

THE MCMANUS

Its name may have changed over the course of its lifetime but The McManus is still one of the best-loved buildings among Dundonians. Dundee's Art Gallery and Museum houses the city's main collections in newly-transformed surroundings.

View south towards Tayport

BROUGHTY FERRY

Once home to Dundee's wealthy jute barons, Broughty Ferry was regarded as 'the richest square mile in Europe'.

Nowadays the appeal of its seaside esplanade and waterfront remains strong. A rich concentration of terrace cafés, bars, restaurants and unusual boutiques makes the four-mile trip east of Dundee's centre all the more rewarding.

Dundee from Broughty Ferry beach

 Tay Rail Bridge

City Centre

We're as passionate about the cities we are in as we are about our hotels.

That's why we commissioned original photographs of each city for our room designs rather than bland wall-fillers. So when you check in to your Apex room in Dundee, Edinburgh or London, you'll always have a sense of where you are in the comfort and quietness of your room.

We hope the images in this book inspire you to find time to explore Dundee or visit some of the buildings and landmarks featured. The flow of the book follows a simple route which you can try for yourself from a starting point at City Quay.

www.apexhotels.co.uk

TEXT BY GORDON MCCULLOCH

THANK YOU TO THE FOLLOWING:
Dundee City Council
Dundee Heritage Trust

PHOTOGRAPHY & BOOK DESIGN BY DAVID SPRINGFORD
Visit David's other photography at www.infinityphotos.co.uk and his design work at www.atomdesign.co.uk